Rising and Falling

By William Matthews

Rising and Falling

Poems by William Matthews

An Atlantic Monthly Press Book

LITTLE, BROWN AND COMPANY   BOSTON   TORONTO

5/1979
am. Lit.

FIRST EDITION

Some of these poems first appeared in the following maga-
zines: *Abraxas, American Poetry Review, Antaeus, Aspen An-
thology, Attaboy!, Atlantic Monthly, Beloit Poetry Journal,
Black Warrior Review, Chowder Review, Epoch, Granite,
Grilled Flowers, Gumbo, Iowa Review, Ironwood, Missouri
Review, Mountain Gazette, Ohio Review, Paris Review,
Quarterly West, Rapport.*

LIBRARY OF CONGRESS CATALOGING IN PUBLICATION DATA
Matthews, William, 1942–
Rising and falling.
I. Title.
PS3563.A855R57   811'.5'4   78-27700
ISBN 0-316-55076-0
ISBN 0-316-55077-9 pbk.

ATLANTIC–LITTLE, BROWN BOOKS
ARE PUBLISHED BY
LITTLE, BROWN AND COMPANY
IN ASSOCIATION WITH
THE ATLANTIC MONTHLY PRESS

Designed by D. Christine Benders

MV

*Published simultaneously in Canada
by Little, Brown & Company (Canada) Limited*

PRINTED IN THE UNITED STATES OF AMERICA

for my father and mother

Faîtes simple.

Escoffier

Notes

In the poems about Bud Powell and Alcide Pavageau I've given Powell a heroin habit and Pavageau (by implication) a limp, for reasons the poems developed. They are not necessarily good biography.

Parts of "Nurse Sharks" are based on (and some phrasing is from) passages in *The Natural History of Sharks*, by Lineaweaver and Backus (Doubleday, 1973).

Table of Contents

I

SPRING SNOW

Here comes the powdered milk I drank
as a child, and the money it saved.
Here come the papers I delivered,
the spotted dog in heat that followed me home

and the dogs that followed her.
Here comes a load of white laundry
from basketball practice, and sheets
with their watermarks of semen.

And here comes snow, a language
in which no word is ever repeated,
love is impossible, and remorse. . . .
Yet childhood doesn't end,

but accumulates, each memory
knit to the next, and the fields
become one field. If to die is to lose
all detail, then death is not

so distinguished, but a profusion
of detail, a last gossip, character
passed wholly into fate and fate
in flecks, like dust, like flour, like snow.

MOVING AGAIN

At night the mountains look like huge
dim hens. In a few geological eras
new mountains may
shatter the earth's shell
and poke up like stone wings.
Each part must serve for a whole.
I bring my sons to the base
of the foothills and we go up.
From a scruff of ponderosa
pines we startle gaudy swerves
of magpies that settle in our rising
wake. Then there's a blooming
prickly pear. "Jesus, Dad, what's that?"
Willy asks. It's like a yellow tulip
grafted to a cactus: it's a beautiful
wound the cactus puts out
to bear fruit and be healed.
If I lived with my sons
all year I'd be less sentimental
about them. We go up
to the mesa top and look down
at our new hometown. The thin air
warps in the melting light
like the aura before a migraine.
The boys are tired. A tiny magpie
fluffs into a pine far below
and farther down in the valley

of child support and lights
people are opening drawers.
One of them finds a yellowing
patch of newsprint with a phone
number penciled on it
from Illinois, from before they moved, before
Nicky was born. Memory
is our root system.
"Verna," he says to himself
because his wife's in another room,
"whose number do you suppose this is?"

SNOW LEOPARDS AT THE DENVER ZOO

There are only a hundred or so
snow leopards alive, and three
of them here. Hours I watch them jump
down and jump up, water being
poured. Though if you fill a glass
fast with water, it rings high to the top,
noise of a nail driven true. Snow
leopards land without sound,
as if they were already extinct.

If I could, I'd sift them
from hand to hand, like a fire,
like a debt I can count but can't pay.
I'm glad I can't. If I tried to
take loss for a wife, and I do,
and keep her all the days of my life,
I'd have nothing to leave my children.
I save them whatever I can keep
and I pour it from hand to hand.

THE PARTY

I don't care if nobody
under forty can hang a door
properly. I'm six and I'm bored.
In the kitchen Lavada
is plucking a turkey
who looks crumpled
and turned inside out.
He's full of holes.
I throw my skinny arms in the air
as far as my bones will let them go
and giggle. It's ten years to Lavada's heart
attack and sixty to mine.
Black overweight Lavada tucks
a feather in her hair
and we dance, her triceps
wobbling like charred wattles. We laugh
until our jawbones sting
as if we'd drunk mossy
cold, rust-flecked water
from the bottom of the well.

A WALK

February on the narrow beach, 3:00
A.M. I set out south. Cape Cod Light
on its crumbling cliff above me turns
its wand of light so steadily
it might be tolling a half-life,
it might be the second-hand
of a schoolroom clock,
a kind of blind radar.

These bluffs deposited by glaciers
are giving themselves away
to the beaches down the line, three
feet of coastline a year. I follow
them south at my own slow pace.
Ahead my grandfather died
in a boat and my father
found him and here I come.

If I cleave to the base of the berm
the offshore wind swirls grit
just over my head and the backwash
rakes it away. If I keep going
south toward my grandfather's house
in Chatham, and beyond,
the longshore current grinds the sand
finer the farther I go. It spreads

it wider and the beaches sift
inland as far as they can go
before beachgrass laces them down
for now. It gets to be spring,
I keep walking, it gets to be
summer. Families loll.
Now the waves are small; they keep
their swash marks close to home.

A little inland from the spurge
and sea-rockets my tan sons kick
a soccer ball north, against
grains that may once have been
compacted to sandstone, then
broken back to grains, bumbling
and driven and free again,
shrinking along the broadening edge.

THE NEWS

From each house on the street,
the blue light of the news.
Someone's dog whirps three times
and scuffs the leaves.
It's quiet, a school night.
The President and his helpers
live at one end of the news,
parents at the other.
The news for today
is tape recordings
of dry ice, sports
for today is weather.
Lights go back into the walls.
These might as well be
my neighbors. The news
uses us all to travel by.
I might as well be one
of their children, bees
sleeping the treaty of honey.
The news will find me soon
enough. I veer between
two of their houses
home through the woods.

STRANGE KNEES

It's one of the ways you see
yourself. Over the snow's blue skin
you go strictly, to honor the slag
of calcium in your knees,
to honor the way you say

Bad Knees, Bad Dog, Bad Luck.
Your sons love to hear how you
collapsed in the lobby
of Cinema II, a latch in your knee
not catching.

               It's true your knees
hurt all the time but your sons dote
wrongly on that fact. They make you Pain's
Firework. They want to know why
they love you and they eat your stories

up. You saved the cat. You're squeaking
home two miles over the moonwashed
snow because your car broke down.
The stories grow crooked inside
you and your knees grow bad.

ISLA MUJERES

The shoal we saw from the boat was fish;
it parted as I dove through, and formed
again overhead, each fish
like a dancing molecule in a rock.
On the flight to Mérida we came down
through clouds that looked like brains
or scrambled eggs, but they were only
wisps and down we came. I'd swim
back up a chimney of fish and break,

already squinting, back into bright air.
If love is curiosity, I loved those fish.
Those nights I ate her, she didn't come
so much as she would go.
Her cunt-lather tasted already of memory
and fever-sped loss, as if I would dream
again and again — and I do —

of falling through her. Sometimes I dream
I'm her, she's me, I'm on my back, she's eating
and falling through me, and as I start
to concentrate and come, my mind
"wanders," as a teacher would say to chide
one of our children, half of whose classmates
come from "broken" homes, should one
of our children stare too long
out a window, imagining he could fly.

LIVING AMONG THE DEAD

There is another world,
but it is in this one.

                    Paul Eluard

First there were those who died
before I was born.
It was as if they had just left
and their shadows would
slip out after them
under the door so recently closed
the air in its path was still
swirling to rest.
Some of the furniture came from them,
I was told, and one day
I opened two chests
of drawers to learn what the dead kept.

But it was when I learned to read
that I began always
to live among the dead.
I remember Rapunzel,
the improved animals
in the *Just-So Stories*, and a flock
of birds that saved themselves
from a hunter by flying in place
in the shape of a tree,

their wings imitating the whisk
of wind in the leaves.

My sons and I are like some wine
the dead have already bottled.
They wish us well, but there is nothing
they can do for us.
Sebastian cries in his sleep,
I bring him into my bed,
talk to him, rub his back.
To help his sons live easily
among the dead is a father's great work.
Now Sebastian drifts, soon he'll sleep.
We can almost hear the dead
breathing. They sound like water
under a ship at sea.

To love the dead is easy.
They are final, perfect.
But to love a child
is sometimes to fail at love
while the dead look on
with their abstract sorrow.

To love a child is to turn
away from the patient dead.
It is to sleep carefully
in case he cries.

Later, when my sons are grown
among their own dead, I can
dive easily into sleep and loll
among the coral of my dreams
growing on themselves

until at the end
I almost never dream of anyone,
except my sons,
who is still alive.

II

LEFT HAND CANYON

for Richard Hugo

The Rev. Royal Filkin preaches
tomorrow on why we are sad.
Brethren, Montana's a landscape
requiring faith: the visible
government arrives in trucks,
if you live out far enough.
If you live in town, the government's
gone, on errands, in trucks.

Let citizens go to meetings,
I'll stay home. I hate a parade.
By the time you get the trout
up through the tiny triangular
holes in the Coors cans, they're so
small you have to throw them back.
Glum miles we go
to Grandmother's house.

The earth out here doesn't bear us
up so much as it keeps us out,
an old trick of the beautiful.
Remember what Chief Left Hand said?
Never mind. Everything else
was taken from him,

let's leave his grief alone.
My Eastern friends ask me

how I like it in the West,
or God's country, as it's sometimes
called, though God, like a slumlord,
lives in the suburbs: Heaven.
And I don't live "in the West";
I live in this canyon among a few
other houses and abandoned
mines, vaccinations that didn't take.

OLD RECORDS

Les shows me his new Braun
tape deck. "After I've played them
three or four times I can hear records
begin to grind down. Now I play
them once, to tape." He's got a wall
of them, uncirculated coins.
Things go by, the summer draining
into the fall; breweries consolidate,
there's a golf course where the woods
were. We're like a fire
and save things from ourselves.
Furtwängler's too-fast fourth movement
that I love, Coltrane breaking
his breath in the hissing rapids,
Janis in heat, Janis in scratch,
Bjørling's beautiful voice
ruined by whisky —
fuzz on the ripe notes and fuzz
continuing to grow.

IN MEMORY OF THE UTAH STARS

Each of them must have terrified
his parents by being so big, obsessive
and exact so young, already gone
and leaving, like a big tipper,
that huge changeling's body in his place.
The prince of bone spurs and bad knees.

The year I first saw them play
Malone was a high school freshman,
already too big for any bed,
14, a natural resource.
You have to learn not to
apologize, a form of vanity.
You flare up in the lane, exotic
anywhere else. You roll the ball
off fingers twice as long as your
girlfriend's. Great touch for a big man,
says some jerk. Now they're defunct
and Moses Malone, boy wonder at 19,
rises at 20 from the St. Louis bench,
his pet of a body grown sullen
as fast as it grew up.

Something in you remembers every
time the ball left your fingertips
wrong and nothing the ball
can do in the air will change that.
You watch it set, stupid moon,

the way you watch yourself
in a recurring dream.
You never lose your touch
or forget how taxed bodies
go at the same pace they owe,
how brutally well the universe
works to be beautiful,
how we metabolize loss
as fast as we have to.

BUD POWELL, PARIS, 1959

I'd never seen pain so bland.
Smack, though I didn't call it smack
in 1959, had eaten his technique.
His white-water right hand clattered
missing runs nobody else would think
to try, nor think to be outsmarted
by. Nobody played as well
as Powell, and neither did he,
stalled on his bench between sets,
stolid and vague, my hero,
his mocha skin souring gray.
Two bucks for a Scotch in this dump,
I thought, and I bought me
another. I was young and pain
rose to my ceiling, like warmth,
like a story that makes us come true
in the present. Each day's
melodrama in Powell's cells
bored and lulled him. Pain loves pain
and calls it company, and it is.

FOUL SHOTS: A CLINIC

for Paul Levitt

Be perpendicular to the basket,
toes avid for the line.

Already this description
is perilously abstract: the ball
and basket are round, the nailhead
centered in the centerplank
of the foul-circle is round,
and though the rumpled body
isn't round, it isn't
perpendicular. You have to draw
"an imaginary line," as the breezy

coaches say, "through your shoulders."
Here's how to cheat: remember
your collarbone. Now the instructions
grow spiritual — deep breathing,
relax and concentrate both; aim
for the front of the rim but miss it
deliberately so the ball goes in.
Ignore this part of the clinic

and shoot 200 foul shots
every day. Teach yourself not to be
bored by any boring one of them.

You have to love to do this, and chances
are you don't; you'd love to be good
at it but not by a love that drives
you to shoot 200 foul shots
every day, and the lovingly unlaunched
foul shots we're talking about now —
the clinic having served to bring us
together — circle eccentrically
in a sky of stolid orbits
as unlike as you and I are
from the arcs those foul shots
leave behind when they go in.

PIANO LESSONS

Sometimes the music is locked
in the earth's body, matter-
of-fact, transforming itself.

So our work could seem useless,
even tautological, as if music
were weather, as if there were never

practice, finger-oil on the keys,
dust in the curtains like the silence
that hates music, parents

to disappoint, small frauds the teacher is paid
to endure but endures for her own
reasons. But the garbled, ill-

believed hymns rise from the piano
on payments. And any God I care for
rakes them in and loves them,

though I don't want to hear
the jokes God makes to love them
unless I be one of those jokes.

LISTENING TO LESTER YOUNG

for Reg Saner

It's 1958. Lester Young minces
out, spraddle-legged as if pain
were something he could step over
by raising his groin, and begins
to play. Soon he'll be dead.
It's all tone now and tone
slurring toward the center
of each note. The edges that used to be
exactly ragged as deckle
are already dead. His embouchure
is wobbly and he's so tired
from dying he quotes himself,
easy to remember the fingering.

It's 1958 and a jazz writer is coming home
from skating in Central Park. Who's that
ahead? It's Lester Young! *Hey Pres,*
he shouts and waves, letting his skates
clatter. *You dropped your shit,* Pres says.

It's 1976 and I'm listening
to Lester Young through stereo equipment
so good I can hear his breath rasp,
water from a dry pond —,

its bottom etched, like a palm,
with strange marks, a language
that was never born
and in which palmists therefore
can easily read the future.

THE BLUE NAP

I slept "like a stone," or like that vast
stone-shaped building, the planetarium.
No dreams I can remember:
the dark unbroken blue
on which the stars will take
their places, like bright sheep

grazing the sparse sky.
The night I share with others is cloudy
as if it were groggy from snowing.
On the plains, the lights of Longmont
waver. I begin to re-invent
my life, turning on lights,

grinding some coffee beans — French roast,
dark enough to shine. The kettle sends up
its flume of steam. The material world is always
swirling away. Six hours ago I lay down
so tired I slept through
an evening I'd have given to basketball

and friends. A snow as dry
as confectioners' sugar has stopped.
I take my dog for a walk
over the sifting fields. To him
it's not midnight. It's dark and snow
smells like the air it's fallen through.

ALCIDE "SLOW DRAG" PAVAGEAU

Walking with Jesus the slow,
behind the beat. Mr. Resistance.
Mr. Ohm, Mr. Exactly Lame.

By some reluctance, some
restraint, if it be a restraint,
by some undertow and stutter,

the halt and lame can strut.
You can hear it yourself. Buy
a few records and think how big

a bass is to a small boy,
his fingers bleeding to grow deft.
Bandages are for amateurs

and they blur the tone, that habit
a bassist and his bass conspire,
the way a couple learns a stride

though the man's taller by a foot.

SKIN DIVING

The snorkel is the easiest woodwind.
Two notes in the chalumeau:
rising and falling.
Here is the skin of sleep,
the skin of reading, surfaces

inseparable from depths.
How far does the light go down?
Wouldn't we like to know.
I love this exact and calm
suspense, the way the spirit is said

to hover above a deathbed,
curious and tender as it is
detached, a cloud on the water,
a cloud in the sky,
as if desire were already

memory. Just as a diction
predicts what we might say
next, an emotion loves its chums.
But here, in poise and in hard thought,
I look down to find myself happy.

III

THE ICEHOUSE, POINTE AU BARIL, ONTARIO

Each vast block in its batter
of sawdust must have weighed
as much as I did. The sweat
we gathered running down
the path began to glaze.
We could see our breaths,
like comic strip balloons
but ragged, grey, opaque.

A warehouse of water on an island.
Once we arrived by seaplane:
the island looked like a green footprint.
Someone in a hurry saved time
by not sinking with each step.

In the icehouse I'd clear my name
on a block of ice and the dank film
of sawdust on my finger was as dense
as parts of grown-up conversation,
the rivalry of uncles and managing
money. The managers I knew
wore baseball caps and yelled.
As for money, I thought it was like food.
When blueberries were in season
we ate them all the time.

I always hoped to find a pickerel
in some block of ice

I was signing. Eyes frozen clear,
the tiny teeth like rasps on a file, the head
tapering to so fine a point it seemed
it could drill its way out. . . .
I'd smear the block clean with both hands cold
white under their gloves of sawdust.
Look here, I'd say clearly.

A SMALL ROOM IN ASPEN

Stains on the casements,
dustmotes, spiderless webs.
No chairs, and a man waking up,
or he's falling asleep.

Many first novels begin
with the hero waking up,
which saves their authors
from writing well about sleep.

His life is the only novel
about him. Mornings
he walks past the park:
Tai Ch'i students practicing

like slow lorises.
A room on the second floor.
He'd dreamed of a ground floor
room, an insistent cat

at the door, its mouth pink
with wrath he couldn't salve
and grew to hate. All afternoon
he's a cloud that can't rain.

There's no ordinary life
in a resort town, he thinks,

though he's wrong: it laces
through the silt of tourists

like worm life. At dusk
the light rises in his room.
A beautiful day, all laziness
and surface, true without

translation. Wherever I go
I'm at home, he thinks,
smug and scared both,
fierce as a secret,

8,000 feet above sea level.
The dark on its way down
has passed him, so he seems
to be rising, after the risen

light, as if he were to keep watch
while the dark sleeps,
as if he and it were each
other's future and children.

TALKING TO THE MOON

A defeated politician is in circulation
again, as we say of coins,
and his mouth is full of words.
His words have all been handled smooth.
They'd shrink, like lozenges, except
some sweat from everyone who's had them
is on them. He could be you,
why don't you support him?

But some people hoard words.
"The year the lake froze all the way
across . . . ," a sentence might begin
and then nod, sleepy in a hot kitchen.
The words are a spell to make the lake
freeze again. The sentence never ends.

Rick used to love to tell how he
and Joanne would creep into her parents'
house after dates, and under
the dining room table he'd eat her
out, he'd say, as if she were an egg
and he a weasel.
His eyes gleamed with grief.
He wanted her back. He told
the story again and again.

The full moon fills the canyon
with pale cream. My huge dog leans

against my knee so hard
he'd fall over if I moved.
Soon he'll go to sleep under the juniper.
The other morning a finch landed on his back
while he slept. He unfurled one eye.
Hmmm, a finch. . . . I tell him his name.
He goes to the juniper and sleeps.

The moon's so bright
it has no features, button with no holes.
I've nothing to say to the moon.
Still, I want to talk.
I want words to be magic,
some secret I have the way I have
my body, so long as it lasts.
I want words to be food,
enough for us all to eat.
The mild stars shine.
The words I want
are sewing my body to sleep,
the no news that is good news, blood
tying and untying its knots.

THE MAIL

The star route man downshifts
his pale purple jeep called a Bronco
instead of a Rat or a Toucan.
The mailbox gets fed. Sharon mutters
out in her sweater, imploring
herself. What about? The wind,
water, the dead current of woodgrain
in the headboard of the bed.
She goes in to open the mail
which mainly says Read Me
I'm Here and See You
Tomorrow, (signed) little ripples
of ink. They make her want
to brush her hair and if it could
her hair would rise to the brush
like a happy pet. She stares
out the window. She could go anywhere.
Though the wind doesn't stop,
nor the light, to write a few words
beginning Dear Sharon, Dear Hair,
Dear Snowgrains Swirled Off The Roof,
Dear Window Pulling Me There.

SUNDAY ALONE IN A FIFTH FLOOR APARTMENT, CAMBRIDGE, MASSACHUSETTS

The *Globe* at the door, a jaunt
to the square for the Sunday *Times*.
Later the path you made has healed,
anyone may use it. A good day

for a fire. Fast clouds tug
their moorings of rain, bent
like a wet field in the wind.
It's almost dusk when you look out,

the sun falling, visible
beneath the curds of clouds.
Open the window. It's like leaving
the door to the shower stall open.

A draft and a few bars
from the Linz Symphony wend
in, like an exact crack in a damp wall
of white noise, the dial tone, the breathing

of sleepers, the dub-dub of a car's left
tires smattering the manhole cover
on Ware St. The music of others
is almost enough, but you can put on

a record to be sure, to make you want

to dance late in the day
in a light that seems to come from inside
the cloud bellies, like the rash that breaks out

just below the skin over a woman's breasts
as orgasm comes on, and on, and goes.

FOUR POEMS ABOUT JAMAICA

1. Montego Bay, 10:00 P.M.

A chandelier, a tiara,
a hive of lights. A cruise ship

is leaving, the S.S. Jesus
again, the only ship that comes

here. If I watch the ship go
long enough I become the ship.

So rather than leave I look away —
because the sea is a foreign country

and I love to travel, but not
like a faltering heart

set on fire and pushed out to sea,
not like a birthday cake.

2. Jamaicans Posing to Be Photographed

Illiterate Esther watched me
closing a book and asked,
*Can you hear from the dead
with that box?* God yes.

Today I take pictures.
My subjects are full dress.
My subjects! As the language
I live by flows through me

it carries so much history
I'm embarrassed, I who believe
in language and distrust
its exact parlor tricks.

Full dress, historical
posture, as if they were running
for office or these were wedding
pictures, since white folks care

about weddings. Somber Ronald,
age three. And Esther, archival,
though the dead don't live in boxes
and nothing keeps in the heat.

3. A Hairpin Turn above Reading, Jamaica

for Russell Banks

Here's where the fire truck fell
beached on its side, off the road.
So when the fire fell into itself
we came down the hill to watch
the fire truck get saved. Only

the rich live this high, with a view
of the bay, and the rich
will be with us forever,

though the pump at the base
of the mountain burns out

and the Socialist party, in power,
is sorry. The rich buy truckloads
of water and hire the poor
to drive them up. Water will go
uphill if money will go down.

Today there's a goat in the bend,
stolid and demure. She'll move
soon: there's nothing to eat in the road.
A cow and two egrets tack
into the shadow of a mango.

It's noon. Above the bay, turkey
buzzards sift the thermals.
At dawn they perch and spread
their wings to dry, like laundry.
My friends and I are the rich,

though the house is rented. We'll fall
away, the goat will loll off the road,
the bad clutch in the van will slur
but we'll make it up, and we do,
heat-steeped, thoughtful, and sleepy.

4. Kingston

No photograph does justice, etc.,
but what does a photograph care
for justice? It wants to be clear,
the way an angel need not mean,
but be, duty enough for an angel.

No angels here. Hovels seen from far
enough away they look picturesque.
The blatant blue sky so cool in pictures
is gritty with heat. The long day stings.
We squint at the lens. Though the lines

in our faces are engraved by the acids
of muscle-habits, not by tears.
Sympathy we have to learn. Here's
a family of three living in a dead car.
The guidebooks warned us away

from this, and so we came,
ungainly, spreading
our understandings of sorrow like wet wings.
We turn and turn, but everywhere is here,
a blurred circle of wing scuffs.

HARVEST

A few rats are gnawing
along the floor of the silo,
but what are a few rats
against this tower of food?
It takes 75,000 crocus blossoms
to make a pound of saffron.

And after today out there
in the heat, nobody dreams of food.
In our dream, Mary Slater
swings higher and higher
on the vine over the Haskins'
creek, and disappears.

OPENING HER JEWEL BOX

She discovers a finish
of dust on the felt drawer-bottoms,
despite the long time
it's been since she opened it
or wore lipstick. Sometimes she's asked
"What are you thinking of?"
and she's so startled she says
"Nothing," rather than describe
a mug with a bite-shaped chip
in its rim, or years ago
killing a cat with carbon monoxide
for love of a medical student.
It thrashed as far from the tailpipe
as the sack would stretch —
ball of fur in a taut lung
that wouldn't work. The cat grew slack
and then grew stiff.
In biology class she'd used corpses
cold from formaldehyde, but
when they cut the cat it was warm
and the heat ran into her wrists.

There used to be two of these earrings.
Erotic memories, how they all
survive, though most of them
need a sentimental past
for a context, or have none,
chunks of space debris

turning in an icy light.
"Nothing in particular,"
she corrects herself out loud,
stunned by the speed of life —
she who used to curse boredom.
"Daddy drive faster," she'd urge
because he wouldn't. Time
to brush my hair, she tells
herself, then time to work.
Her hair pouts in clumps.
It's always been thin, slow
to unsnarl. Easy does it.
She begins to sing, softly at first.

A LIFE OF CRIME

Frail friends, I love you all!
Maybe that's the trouble,
storm in the eye of a storm.
Everyone wants too much.
Instead we gratefully accept
some stylized despair:

suitcoats left hanging
on folding chairs, snow falling
inside a phone booth, cows
scouring some sad pasture.
You know the sort of landscape,
all sensibility and no trees.

Nothing but space, a little
distance between friends.
As if loneliness didn't make us
responsible, and want accomplices.
Better to drink at home
than to fall down in bars.

Or to read all night a novel
with missing heirs, 513 pages
in ten-point type, and lay my body
down, a snarl of urges
orbited by blood,
dreaming of others.

TAKING THE TRAIN HOME

1.

Dusk grew on the window.
I'd listen for the click
of the seams in the rails
to come at the same speed
the telephone wires sagged
and then shot upward to the pole.
All night I slept between
the rails, a boy on a stretcher.
When I'd wake up outside
Chillicothe I felt like a fish.
Alfalfa and cows peered in
as I went by in my
aquarium, my night
in glass. Dawn flew against
my window the same way
a fly swarms by itself
against the heat of a bare
light bulb, like a heart attack.
I'd be home soon, 7:15,
all out for Cincinnati.

2.

It's Sunday and I'm only four
and my grandparents are taking

me to Sharonville, to the roundhouse.
Pop drives. The part in the white crest
of his hair is like a compass needle.
Non sings. From the back seat
I lean between them, I can
feel the soot, the cinders
like black popcorn under my feet.
The roundhouse ceiling is charred
by sparks, and grime
smears its highest windows.
Coalcars smolder on sidings
while the engine turns
away from its arrival.

I was going to live in a roundhouse
when I grew up, a lighthouse.
Every morning the moon
would steam in over the sea
and turn around.
The table would be set for breakfast
before I went to bed,
my little tower of pills
beside the juice glass.
My hair would be white, like Pop's,
and by its light the ships,
long pods of sleep and fuel oil,
coffee beans, brooms
with real straw,
by the light of my hair
ships would sleep into port
and germinate.

3.

In my dream I'm only four

again, Pop is alive.
He walks slowly — emphysema.
I've eaten something
metallic, something
I don't understand.
I circle away from him
to vomit among roadside weeds.
I force it up.
It's like gruel, with roofing nails
for lumps.
I love this dying man.
I look up and he bobs over a wave
in the road, he's swimming
out to sea. I begin
following but my legs are too short,
death is my father,
this is my body
which will fall apart.
I'm sleeping on the ocean.
I'm asleep on a train
outside Red Lion, Ohio.
I don't know; I can't tell,
but it seems to me
that if I could watch my body sleep
it would glow,
growing its antibodies
to eternal life,
growing the lives we give away
when we wake.

IV

A ROADSIDE NEAR ITHACA

Here we picked wild strawberries,
though in my memory we're neither here
nor missing. Or I'd scuff out
by myself at dusk, proud
to be lonely. Now everything's
in bloom along the road at once:
tansy mustard, sow thistle,
fescue, burdock, soapwort,
the mailbox-high day lilies,
splurges of chicory with thin,
ragged, sky-blue flowers.
Or they're one blue the sky
can be, and always, not
varium et mutabile semper,
restless forever. In memory,
though memory eats its banks
like any river, you can carry
by constant revision
some loved thing: a stalk of mullein
shaped like a what's-the-word-for
a tower of terraced bells, that's it,
a carillon! A carillon ringing
its mute changes of pollen into a past
we must be about to enter,
the road's so stained by the yellow
light (same yellow as the tiny
mullein flowers) we shared
when we were imminent.

WAKING AT DUSK FROM A NAP

In the years that pass through
an afternoon's dream, like tape
at Fast Forward, there are
syllables, somehow, in the waterfall,
and in the dream I hear them each
clearly, a classroom
of children reciting their names.
I am not in the dream; it's as if I am
the dream, in which such distinctions
go without saying. And in which
a confusion I may soon have — did I
wake at dawn or dusk? — seems
anticipated: a strand of stars
goes by, like elephants spliced
trunk-to-tail in children's books
or ivory carvings, and the dream won't say
if they're through for the night
or amiably headed for work.

And the dream — and once, I remember,
it seemed I was the dream —
the dream tilts up to pour me out.

For an instant when I wake
there's a whir, perhaps of props
and stagehands, and a laggard star
scrambles over the transom.
The grainy world with its sworls

and lesions, its puckering dusk light,
its dimming patina, its used and casual
beauty, reassembles itself exactly.
And I climb down from bed, gather
my spilled book from the floor,
and watch the lights come on
in the valley, like bright type
being set in another language.

EYES:

the only parts of the body the same
size at birth as they'll always be.
"That's why all babies are beautiful,"
Thurber used to say as he grew
blind — not dark, he'd go on
to explain, but floating in a pale
light always, a kind of candlelit
murk from a sourceless light.
He needed dark to see:
for a while he drew on black
paper with white pastel chalk
but it grew worse. Light bored
into his eyes but where did it go?
Into a sea of phosphenes,
along the wet fuse of some dead
nerve, it hid everywhere and couldn't
be found. I've used up
three guesses, all of them
right. It's like scuba diving, going down
into the black cone-tip that dives
farther than I can, though I dive
closer all the time.

IN MEMORY OF W. H. AUDEN

1.

His heart made a last fist.
The language has used him
well and passed him through.
We get what he collected.
The magpie shines, burns
in the face of the polished stone.

2.

His was a mind alive by a pure greed
for reading, for the book
which "is a mirror,"
as Lichtenberg said: "if an ass
peers into it, you can't expect
an apostle to look out."

It was a mediating mind.
There were the crowds like fields of waving wheat
and there was the Rilkean fire
he didn't like
at the bottom of the night.
He loomed back and forth.
The space shrank.
The dogs of Europe wolved

about the house,
darks defining a campfire.

3.

My friend said Auden died
because his face
invaded his body.
Under the joke is a myth —
we invent our faces:
the best suffer most and it shows.
But what about the face
crumpled by a drunk's Buick?
Or Auden's
face in its fugue of photographs
so suddenly resolved?
It isn't suffering that eats us.

4.

They were not painting about suffering,
the Old Masters. Not the human heart but
Brueghel turns the plowman away
for compositional reasons
and smooths the waters for a ship he made
expensive and delicate.
The sun is implied by how
the sure hand makes the light fall
as long as we watch the painting.
The sure hand is cruel.

SNOW FALLING THROUGH FOG

This is how we used to imagine
the ocean floor: a steady snow of dead
diatoms and forams drifting
higher in the sunken plains, a soggy
dust on the climbing underwater
peaks. But such a weather

would build a parched earth,
a ball of salt. Down the last mountains
above sea level real snow would sift
until it met the rising tide
of salt and the earth was perfect, done.
Now we think of the ocean floor
as several floors, vast plates

grinding against each other as metaphors
grind each other. We say "plates"
as if somewhere the earth
were flat, or we were
faithful to the way our round eyes
flatten the round earth whenever the lack

of a compelling metaphor gives us a chance.
The basins would never fill up
even with our bad ideas.
Information keeps our senses linked.
The fog thins and we can see
more of the air the snow defines,
the snow like a syllabus of starfish.

OUTER SPACE

If you could turn the moon
on a lathe, you would
because you are curious.

And that would explain
why the moon slivers,
but explain it stupidly

by not taking care
to ask how the moon rounds.
And so we go, stupid ideas

for feet. *The better to wander
with*, retort the feet,
and what can you say,

you who shaved those taut
spirals from the moon,
kinks of tightening light

that fell away from your attention
to your work growing smaller
the better you did it?

Threads on a screw, the worm
of a corkscrew, the circular
staircase to sleep. . . .

Soon the moon is gone
as far as it can go and still come back.
Soon there'll be no room

for you: the moon will be all
stomach, like a melon.
The nest you've been meaning

to leave is inside, aslosh with seeds.
Around the outside you curl
like the sky that goes away forever.

NURSE SHARKS

Since most sharks have no flotation bladders and must swim
to keep from sinking, they like to sleep in underwater caves,
wedged between reef-ledges, or in water so shallow
that their dorsal fins cut up from the surf.
Once I woke a nurse shark (so named because it was
thought to protect its young by taking them
into its mouth). It shied from the bubbles I gave up
but sniffed the glint the murky light made on my regulator.

My first shark at last. I clenched
every pore I could. A shark's sense of smell
is so acute and indiscriminate that a shark crossing
the path of its own wound is rapt.
Once a sharp got caught, ripped open by the hook.
The fisherman threw it back after it flopped
fifteen minutes on deck, then caught it again
on a hook baited with its own guts.

Except for the rapacious great white
who often bites first, sharks usually nudge
what they might eat. They're scavengers and like
food to be dead or dying. Move to show you're alive
but not so much as to cause panic: that's what the books
advise. The nurse shark nibbled at my regulator
once, a florid angelfish swam by, the shark
veered off as if it were bored. Its nubbled skin

scraped my kneecap, no blood
but the rasped kneecap pink for a week.

Another year I swam past a wallow of nurse sharks asleep
in three feet of water, their wedge-shaped heads lax
on each other's backs. One of them slowly thrashed
its tail as if it were keeping its balance in the thicket
of sharks sleeping like pick-up-sticks. Its tail sent
a small current over me, a wet wind.
I swirled around a stand of coral and swam
fast to shore, startling the sharks to a waking frenzy:
moil, water opaque with churned-up sand,
grey flames burning out to sea. Last time I go diving
alone, I promised myself, though I lied.

BEDTIME

Usually I stay up late, my time
alone. Tonight at 9:00 I can tell
I'm only awake long enough
to put my sons to bed.
When I start to turn off lights
the boys are puzzled. They're used
to entering sleep by ceding to me
their hum and fizz, the way they give me
50¢ to hold so they can play
without money. I'm their night-light.
I'm the bread baked while they sleep.
And I can scarcely stand up, dry
in the mouth and dizzied
by fatigue. From our rooms
we call back and forth the worn
magic of our passwords and let one
another go. In the morning Sebastian
asks who was the last to fall
asleep and none of us cares or knows.

LONG

for Stanley Plumly

It's about to be too late.
Every shred of the usual weather
is precious and sexual as it goes,
the way the links of a fugue become
one another's strict abandonments.

As for the future, it will not swerve.
Fire sleeps in the tree. Which tree?
Fire sleeps without dreaming and cannot
say. If we call the future's name
it becomes our name, by echo.

And from the dead, not even
a plea that we leave them
alone, each dead locked
in its dead name. If the dead complained,
they would say we summon them poorly,

dull music and thin wine, nor love
enough for the many we make,
much less for the melted dead

in their boxes. Above them
we talk big, since the place is vast

and bland if we tire of looking closely,
washed bland by light from what light
lets us see, our study,
the scripture of matter,
our long narcosis of parting.